piano
All the Way!

Level 3

by
William Gillock

WILLIS MUSIC

HAL•LEONARD®

T0079560

PIANO ALL THE WAY

(Level Three)

Foreword

Level Three of PIANO ALL THE WAY introduces the following concepts in

THEORY:

1. Expanded reading range of

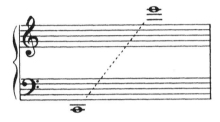

2. Speed drills in note recognition.

3. The 𝅗𝅥. in quarter time.

4. All major and minor scales and their key signatures.

5. Accidentals.

6. Triplet rhythm patterns in quarter time.

7. Grace notes.

8. Syncopation.

TECHNIC:

1. Extensions of 6ths, 7th and octaves.

2. Scale fingering.

3. Legato thirds.

4. The soft pedal.

5. Sforzando and percussive accent touches.

INTERPRETATION:

1. Expanded vocabulary of tempo and mood indications.

2. Balance of melody and accompaniment.

3. Style and mood variety.

W. M. Co. 9586

Unit 1

LEARNING TO RECOGNIZE 5 Cs and 4 Gs

NOTE RECOGNITION DRILLS

MEET THE Cs

MEET THE Gs

Be able to WRITE FROM MEMORY the 5 Cs and 4 Gs at your next lesson.

Remove the inserted page from the back of the book and follow instructions.

W. M. Co., 9586

All other notes that you will need to learn are either a STEP (interval of a 2nd) or a SKIP (interval of a 3rd) up or down from the 5 Cs and 4 Gs.

1. Check all the Cs in this piece.
2. On the keyboard, play and name a 2nd up from all Cs; a 3rd up.

UP FROM C

1. Check all the Cs in this piece.
2. On the keyboard, play and name a 2nd down from all Cs; a 3rd down.

DOWN FROM C

1. Check all the Gs in this piece.
2. On the keyboard, play and name a 2nd up from all Gs; a 3rd up.

UP FROM G

1. Check all the Gs in this piece.
2. On the keyboard, play and name a 2nd down from all Gs; a 3rd down.

DOWN FROM G

W. M. Co., 9586

4

UP AND DOWN FROM C

UP AND DOWN FROM G

AN OLD TUNE
(All Over the Keyboard)

R.H. plays Up - stems
L.H. plays Down-stems

TEST

On the chalk board (or in your manuscript book) write the Cs and Gs your teacher will play on the keyboard. Look carefully to see exactly which keys are being played.

Write 2nds up and down from your notes; 3rds.

THE TUBA PLAYER

Moderato

W. M. Co., 9586

6

THE HARPIST

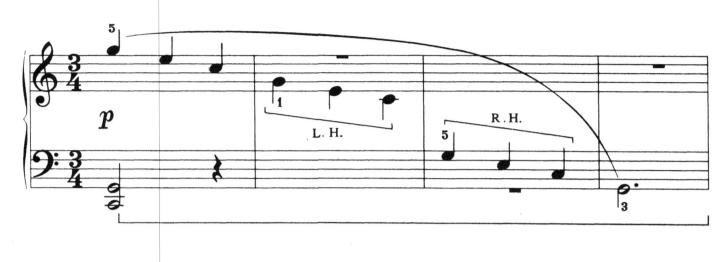

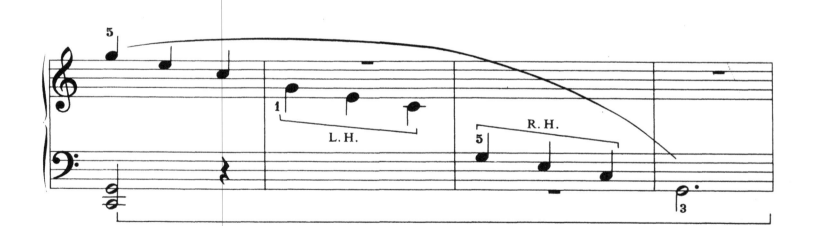

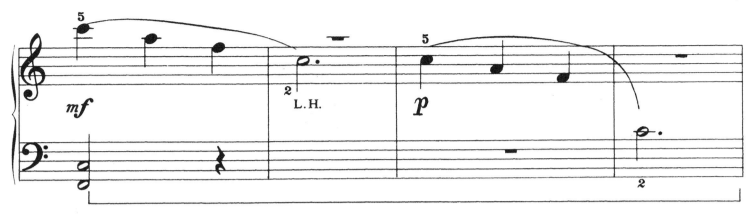

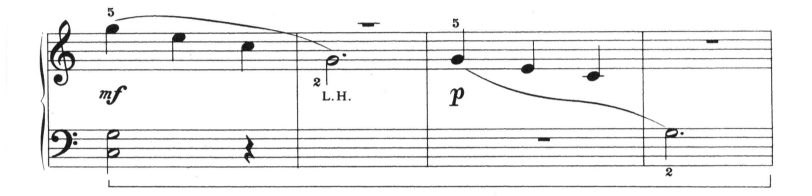

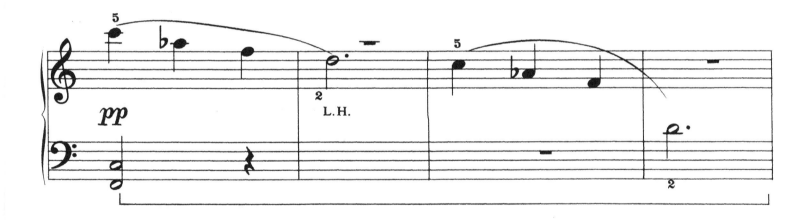

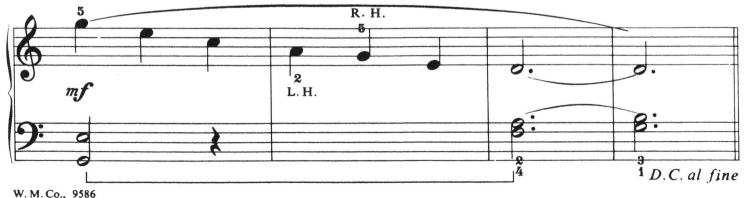

W. M. Co., 9586

A NEW RHYTHM PATTERN

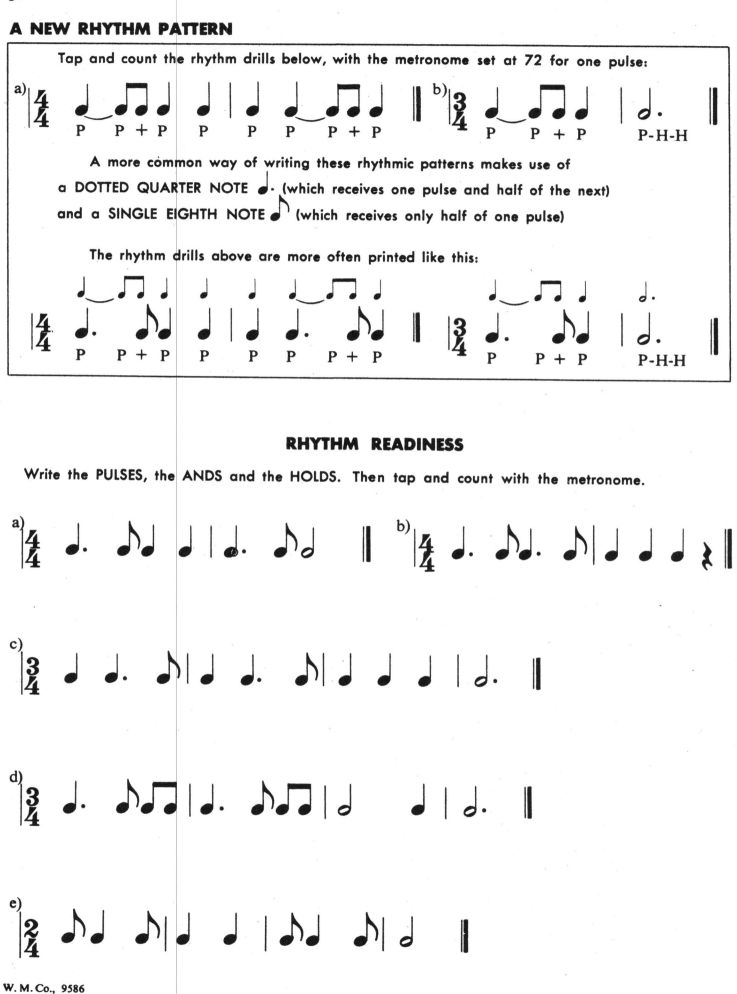

Tap and count the rhythm drills below, with the metronome set at 72 for one pulse:

A more common way of writing these rhythmic patterns makes use of

a DOTTED QUARTER NOTE (which receives one pulse and half of the next)

and a SINGLE EIGHTH NOTE (which receives only half of one pulse)

The rhythm drills above are more often printed like this:

RHYTHM READINESS

Write the PULSES, the ANDS and the HOLDS. Then tap and count with the metronome.

TOY SOLDIER

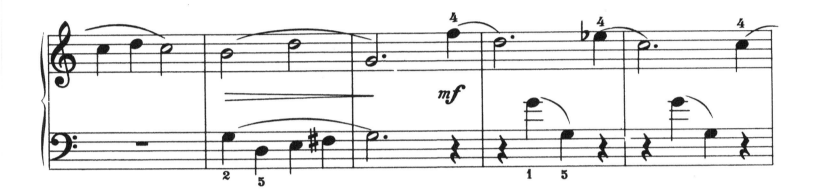

W. M. Co., 9586

PLAYFUL PUPPY

Allegro (Happily — faster than spiritoso)

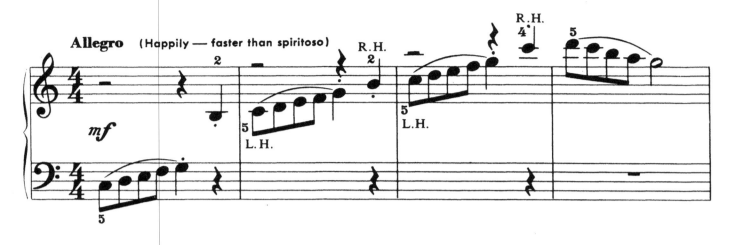

Fine

D.C. al Fine

W. M. Co., 9586

RUSSIAN DANCE

Unit 2

MAJOR AND MINOR SCALES

Play the following scales, first with R.H. (fingering above the notes); then with L.H. (fingering below the notes).

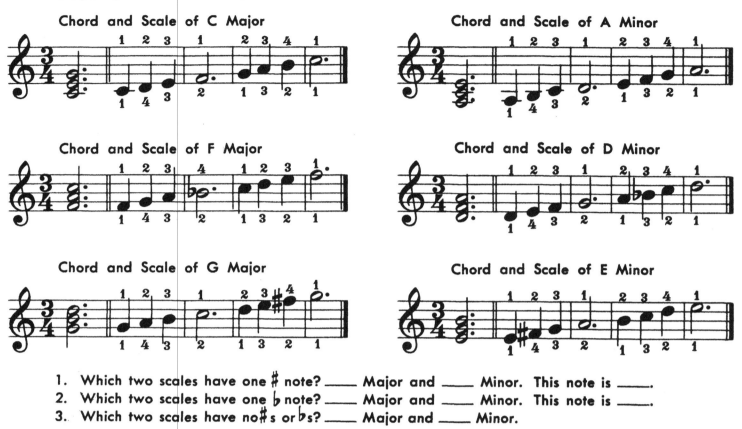

Chord and Scale of C Major

Chord and Scale of A Minor

Chord and Scale of F Major

Chord and Scale of D Minor

Chord and Scale of G Major

Chord and Scale of E Minor

1. Which two scales have one ♯ note? _____ Major and _____ Minor. This note is _____.
2. Which two scales have one ♭ note? _____ Major and _____ Minor. This note is _____.
3. Which two scales have no ♯s or ♭s? _____ Major and _____ Minor.

KEY SIGNATURE

The ♯s and ♭s of scales are usually not printed directly in front of the notes, as they are in the scales above.

Instead, they are printed at the beginning of each staff, and you must remember which notes are played ♯ or ♭. ***THIS IS CALLED THE KEY SIGNATURE***

F MAJOR SCALE

Key signature of 1♭

D MINOR SCALE

Key signature of 1♭

Name the line of the staff which passes through the curved part of the ♭.
All notes that have this **name** must be played ♭.

G MAJOR SCALE

Key signature of 1♯

E MINOR SCALE

Key signature of 1♯

Name the line of the staff which passes through the heavy cross bars of the ♯.
All notes that have this name must be played ♯.

PIECES ALSO HAVE KEY SIGNATURES——

because a piece is usually composed with the notes and chords of one scale.

The following piece has a key signature of 1 _____.
There are two scales that have this key signature: _____ Major and _____ Minor.

In order to tell if a piece is composed in a major or a minor key, you must let your ear help. ARE THE **SOUNDS** MAJOR OR MINOR?

The LOWEST note of the last measure of a piece is usually the letter name of the key in which the piece is composed. (Test this rule now.)

Before you play this piece, check the notes which must be played♯.

MOUNTAIN BALLAD

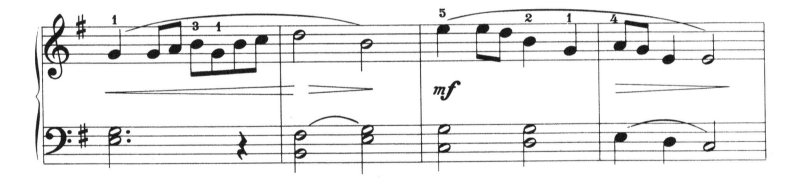

Name the key in which this piece is composed: _____

W. M. Co., 9586

ON MY WAY

The key signature of this piece is 1____ which indicates either ____ Major or ____ Minor.
Name the key.

The ♯, ♭ and ♮ signs which are not in the key signature are called ACCIDENTALS.
The next bar line cancels all accidentals.

The minor scales which you have learned are called PURE MINOR (or SIGNATURE MINOR) because they use only the notes of the key signature. A variation of the minor scale, called the HARMONIC MINOR, is formed by raising the 7th tone of the PURE MINOR a half step.

Scale of A Minor (Harmonic form)

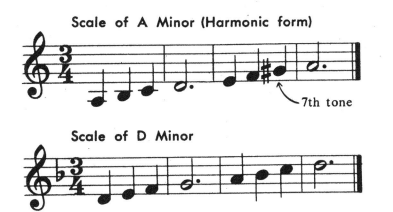

7th tone

Change to the Harmonic form the scales of D Minor and E Minor.

The raised 7th tone of the Harmonic Minor is always written as an accidental.

Scale of D Minor

Scale of E Minor

SPOOKY NIGHT

What is the key signature? Name the key.

Allegretto

W. M. Co., 9586

ALLEGRO IN _____
(Name the Key.)

COUNTRY DANCE

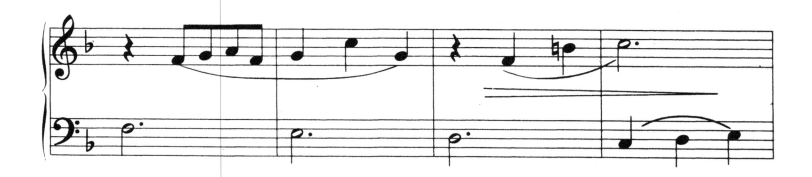

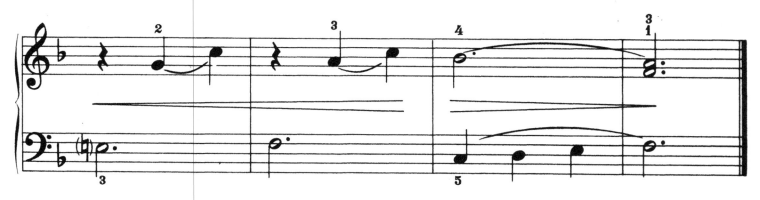

BY A FOREST POOL

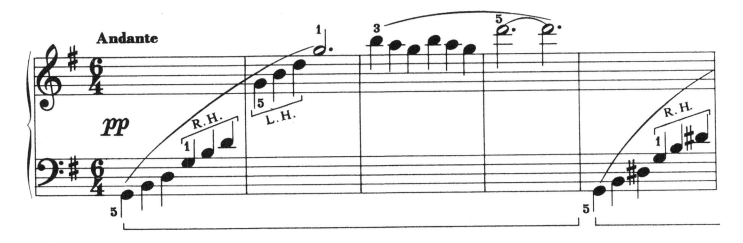

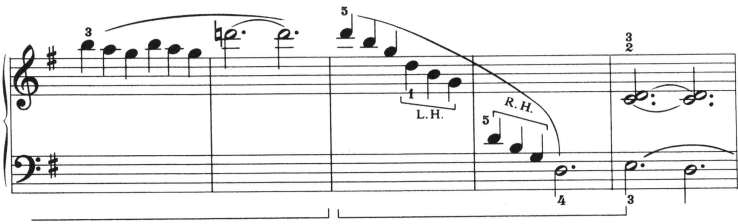

W. M. Co., 9586

Unit 3

THE SHARP KEY SIGNATURES

| 1 Sharp | 2 Sharps | 3 Sharps | 4 Sharps | 5 Sharps | 6 Sharps | 7 Sharps |

G Major or E Minor | D Major or B Minor | A Major or F♯ Minor | E Major or C♯ Minor | B Major or G♯ Minor | F♯ Major or D♯ Minor | C♯ Major or A♯ Minor

AN EASY RULE TO DETERMINE THE KEY IN THE ♯ SIGNATURES:

The first note up (a half tone on the keyboard) from the last sharp, is the name of the major key.

The first note down (a whole tone on the keyboard) from the last sharp, is the name of the minor key. (If this note is sharp in the key signature, the name of the minor key is "Sharp", also.)

TEST THIS RULE WITH THE KEY SIGNATURES ABOVE

The following piece has a key signature of 2 _____ which indicates either _____ Major or _____ Minor. Check the lowest note of the last measure to help determine the key name.

BLACK CATS

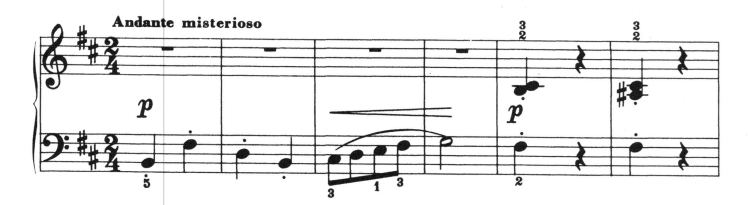

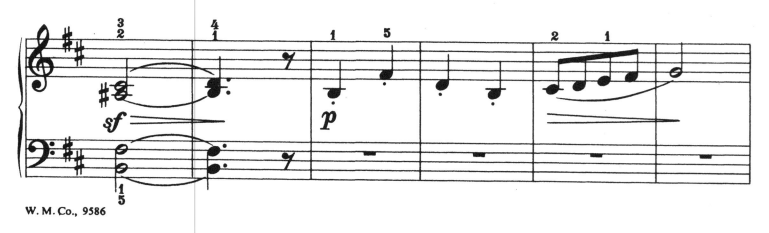

ETUDE IN THIRDS

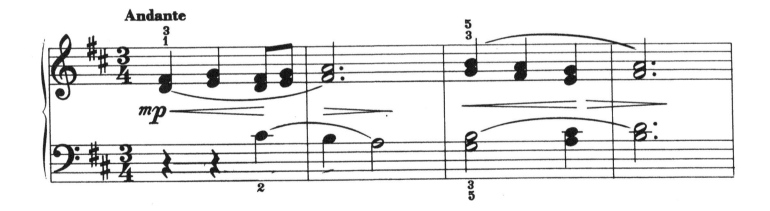

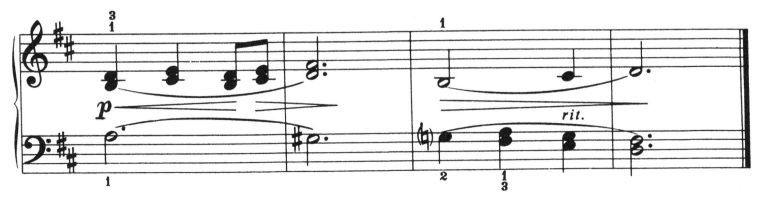

W. M. Co., 9586

Play the scales below, first with R.H.; then with L.H.

Chord and Scale of D Major

Chord and Scale of B Minor

Chord and Scale of A Major

Chord and Scale of F♯ Minor

Chord and Scale of E Major

Chord and Scale of C♯ Minor

1. Which scales have a key signature of 2♯s? —— Major and —— Minor.
2. Which scales have a key signature of 3♯s? —— Major and —— Minor.
3. Which scales have a key signature of 4♯s —— Major and —— Minor.

How can you change the Pure Minor scales to Harmonic Minor?

VILLAGE DANCE

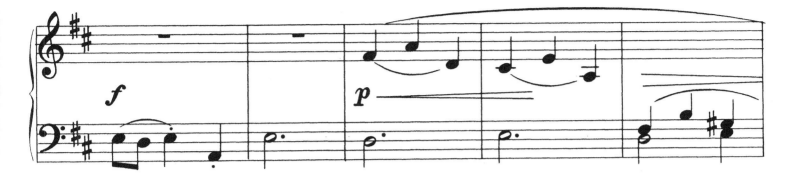

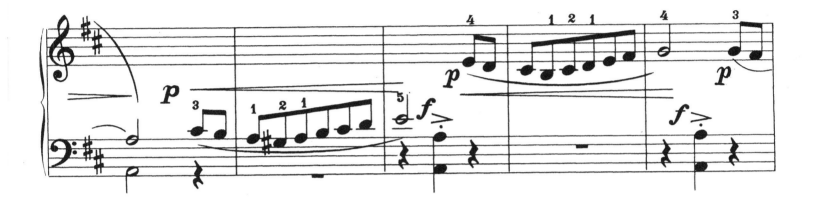

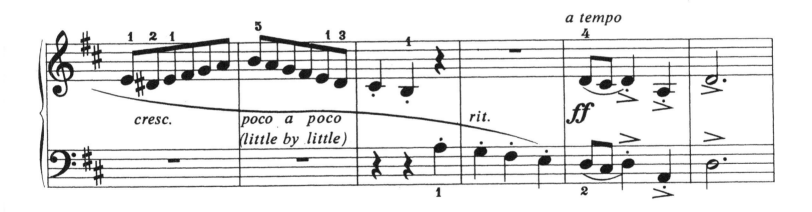

RIDING THE RANGE

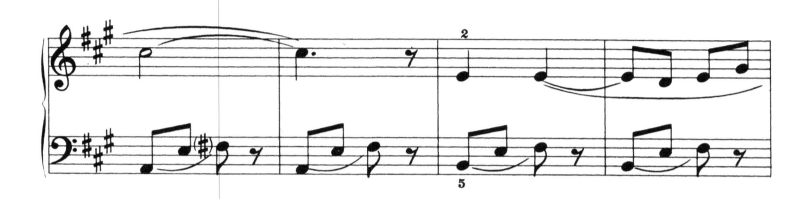

Non

THE BELL TOWER

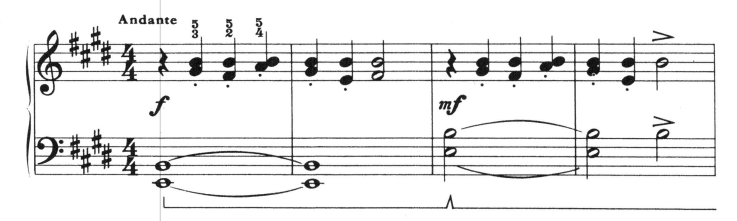

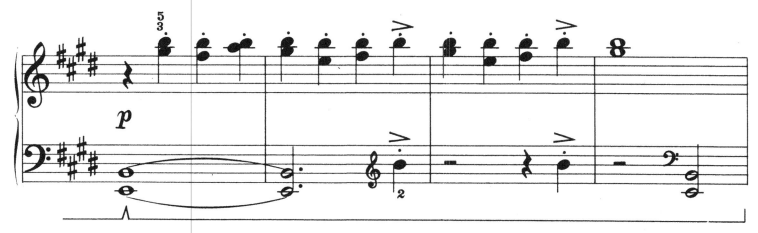

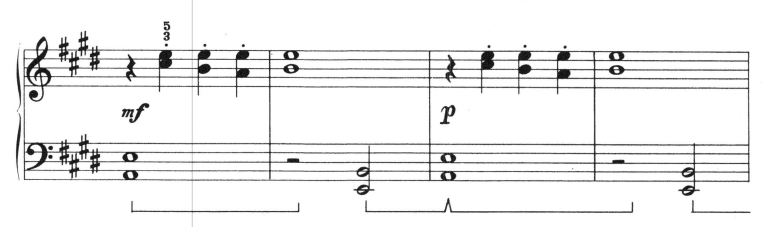

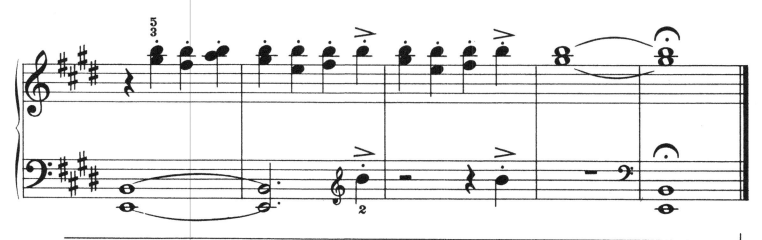

WITCH IN THE FOREST

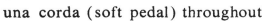

una corda (soft pedal) throughout

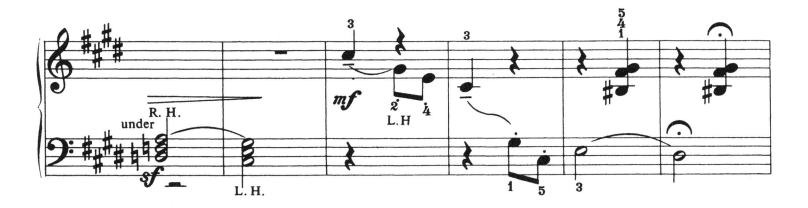

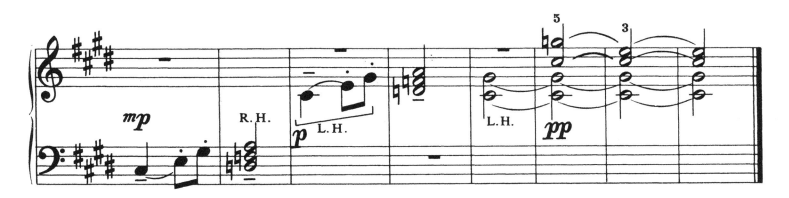

Unit 4

A NEW RHYTHM PATTERN

Three eighth notes printed on one beam 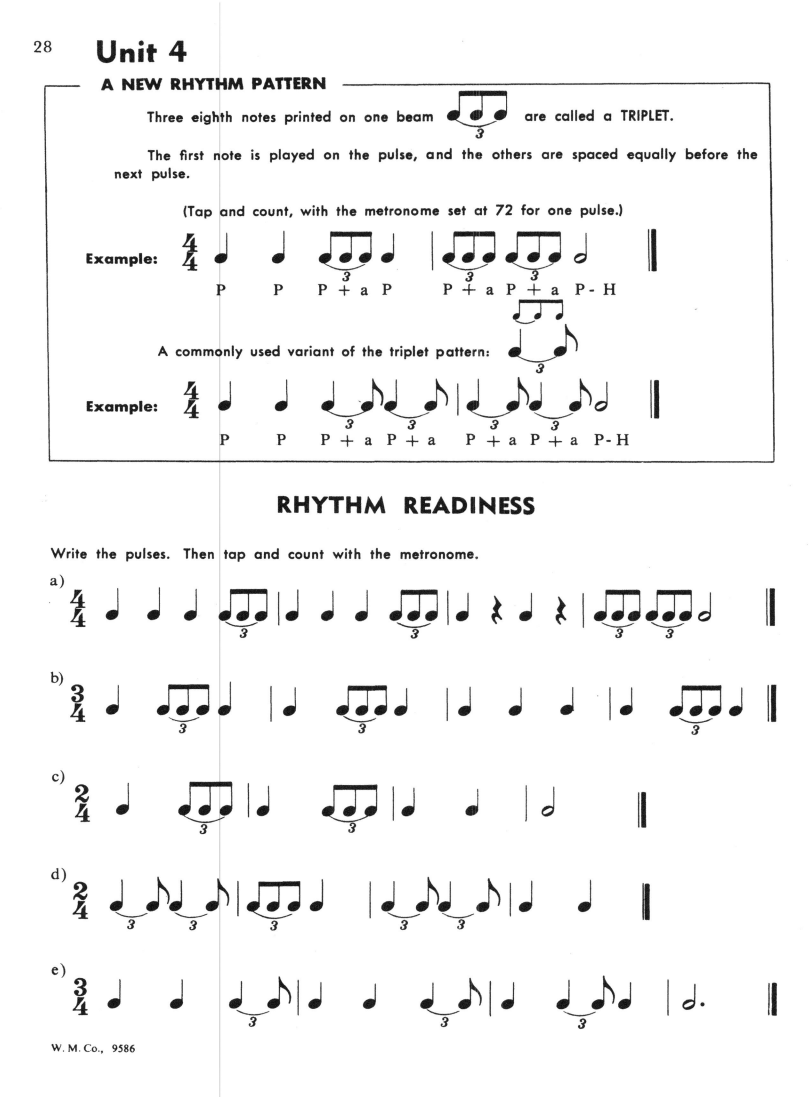 are called a TRIPLET.

The first note is played on the pulse, and the others are spaced equally before the next pulse.

(Tap and count, with the metronome set at 72 for one pulse.)

Example:

P   P   P + a P   P + a P + a P-H

A commonly used variant of the triplet pattern:

Example:

P   P   P + a P + a   P + a P + a P-H

RHYTHM READINESS

Write the pulses. Then tap and count with the metronome.

a)

b)

c)

d)

e)

W. M. Co., 9586

STATELY PROCESSION

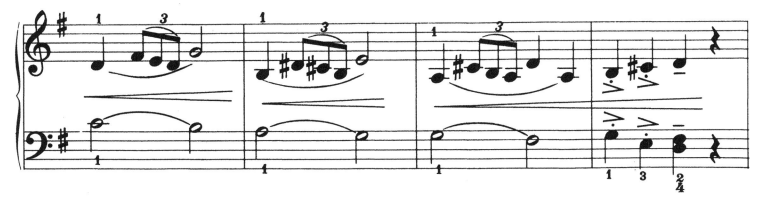

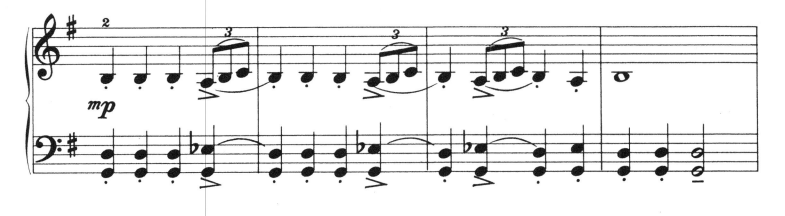

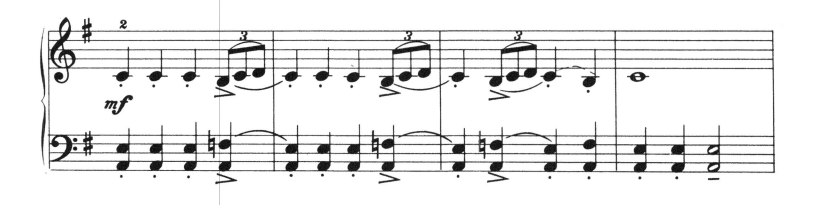

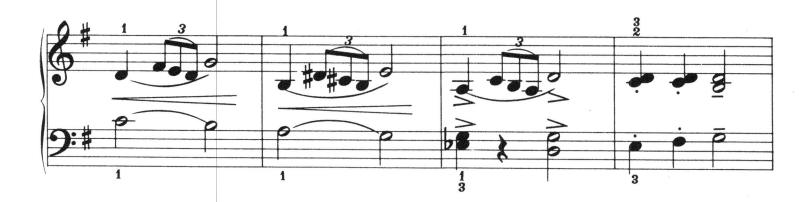

ROCKING CHAIR BLUES

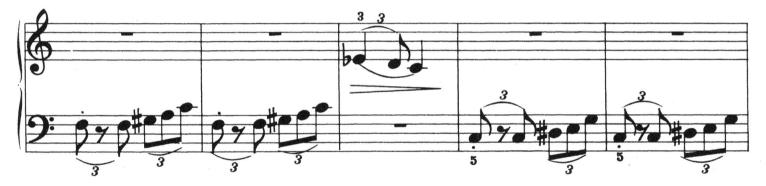

W. M. Co., 9586

32

THE FLAT KEY SIGNATURES

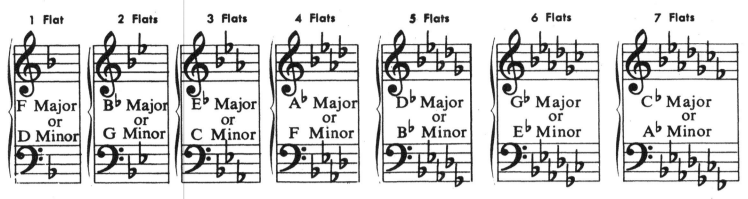

1 Flat	2 Flats	3 Flats	4 Flats	5 Flats	6 Flats	7 Flats
F Major or D Minor	B♭ Major or G Minor	E♭ Major or C Minor	A♭ Major or F Minor	D♭ Major or B♭ Minor	G♭ Major or E♭ Minor	C♭ Major or A♭ Minor

AN EASY RULE TO DETERMINE THE KEY IN THE ♭ SIGNATURES

When there are two or more flats, the name of the major key is the name of the NEXT-TO-LAST flat.

The name of the minor key is always a skip down from the NEXT-TO-LAST flat. (If this note is flat in the key signature, the name of the minor key is "Flat", also.)

TEST THIS RULE WITH THE KEY SIGNATURES ABOVE.

You must memorize the names of the major and minor keys with a signature of only 1♭.

A LIVELY DANCE

Vivace (Lively)

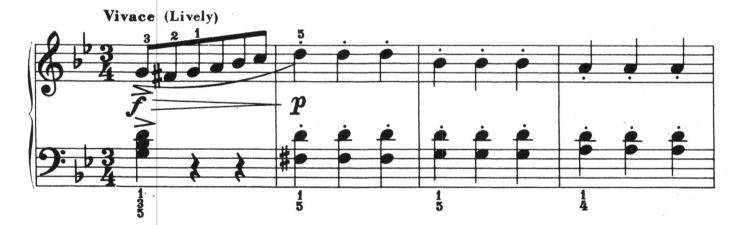

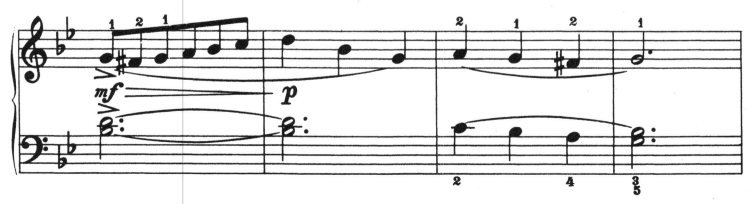

W. M. Co., 9586

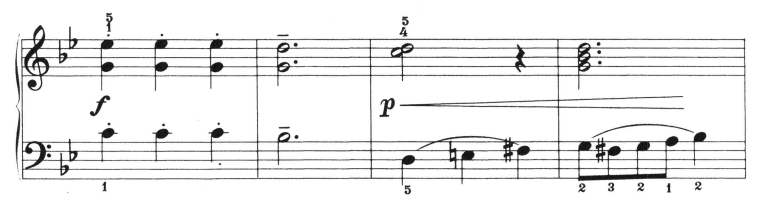

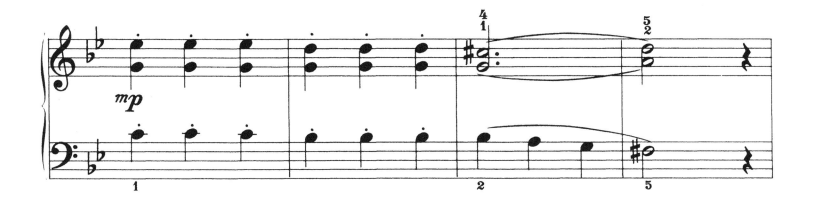

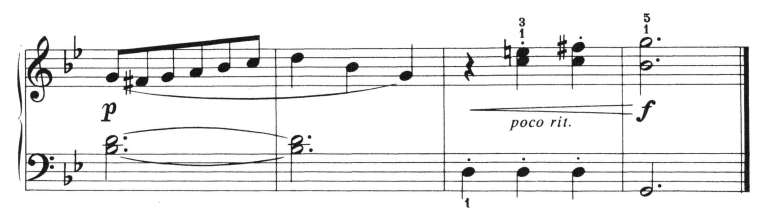

SONG

Andante cantabile (singing)

GHOST DANCE

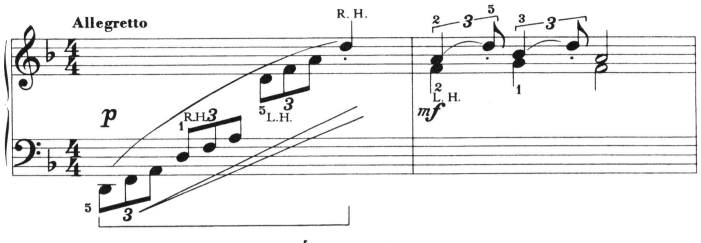

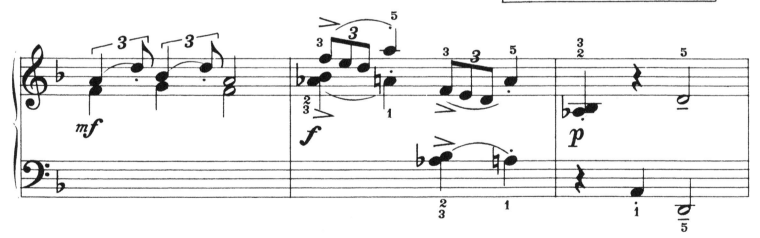

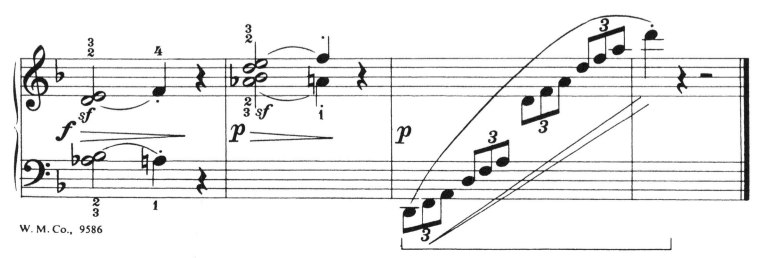

Unit 5

MORE MAJOR AND MINOR SCALES

Play the scales below, first with R.H.; then with L.H.

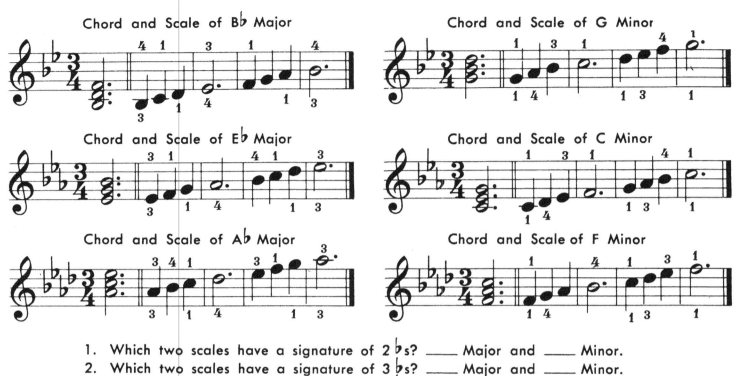

1. Which two scales have a signature of 2 ♭s? _____ Major and _____ Minor.
2. Which two scales have a signature of 3 ♭s? _____ Major and _____ Minor.
3. Which two scales have a signature of 4 ♭s? _____ Major and _____ Minor.

How can you change the Pure Minor scales to Harmonic Minor?

STORMY WEATHER

W. M. Co., 9586

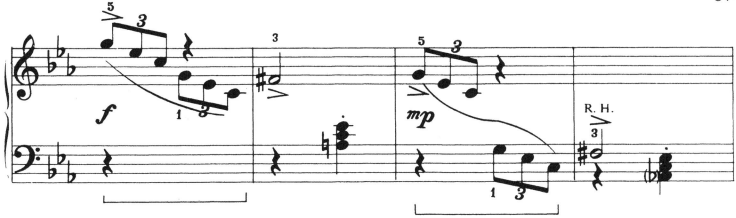

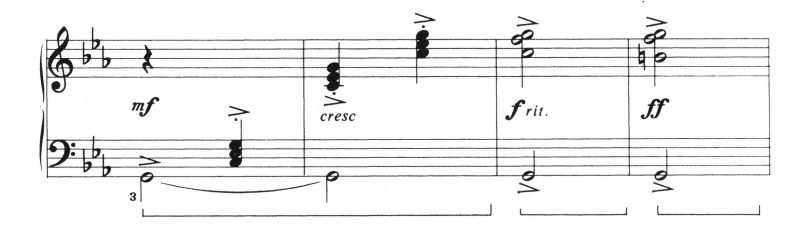

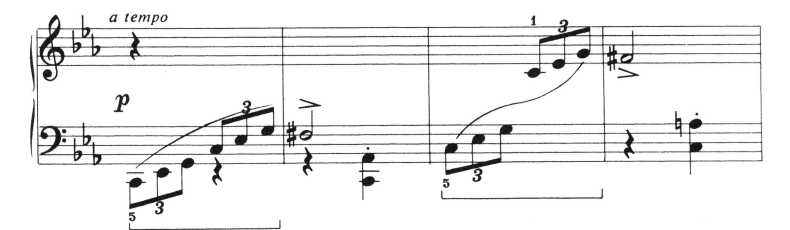

A grace note (♪) has no time value. It is slurred quickly into the large note which always follows.

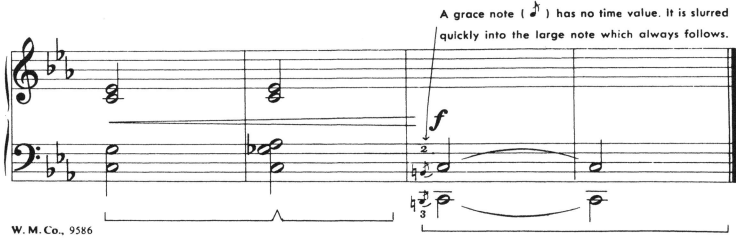

W. M. Co., 9586

ON ROLLER SKATES

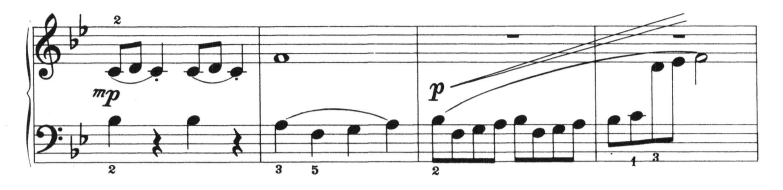

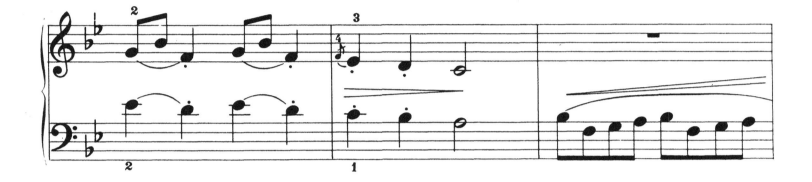

BELLS ACROSS THE LAGOON

* with a little motion
W. M. Co., 9586

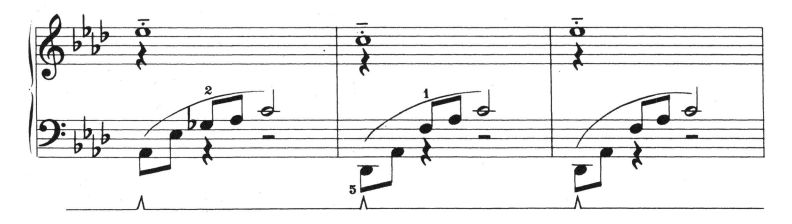

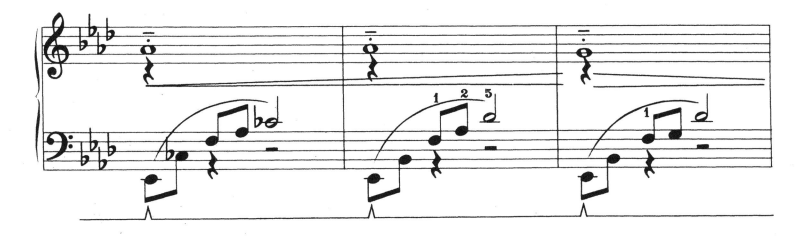

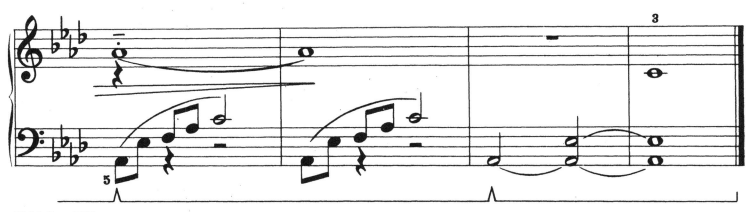

W. M. Co., 9586

Unit 6

THE ENHARMONIC SCALES

Scales which use EXACTLY the same keys on the piano and sound EXACTLY alike, but use different notes and key signatures are called ENHARMONIC SCALES.

There are three pairs of ENHARMONIC MAJOR SCALES
and three pairs of ENHARMONIC MINOR SCALES

1. When you change the Pure Minor scales to Harmonic Minor, if the 7th tone is already sharp you must use the DOUBLE SHARP SIGN (✗) to raise this tone another half step.

2. If the 7th tone is flat, what sign is used to raise it a half step? _____

STEP BY STEP

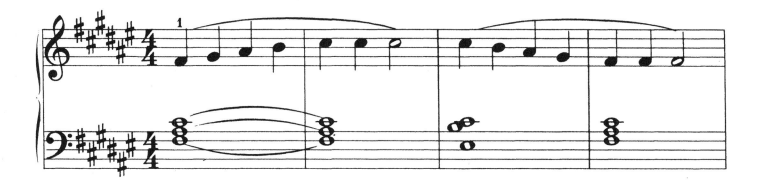

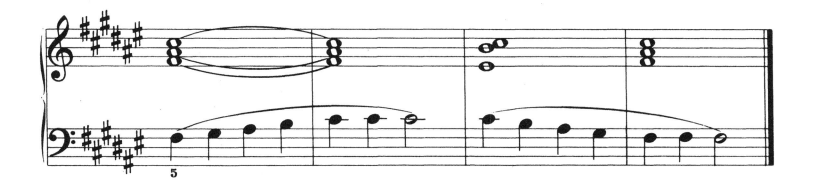

STEP BY STEP

W. M. Co., 9586

∧ Percussive accent

TRUMPET FANFARE

Tempo di marcia

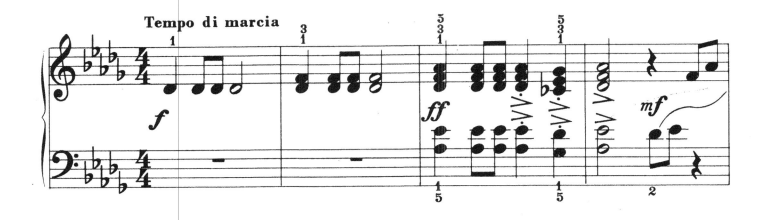

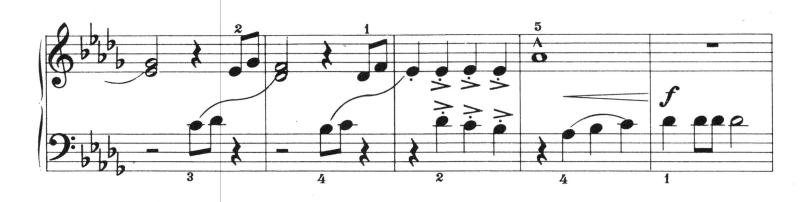

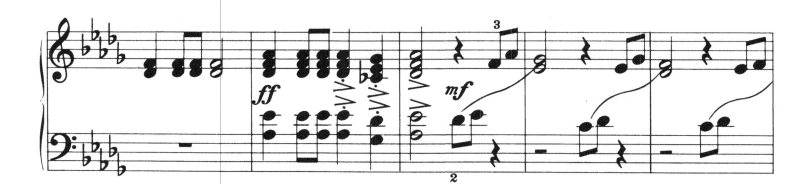

SUMMER CLOUDS

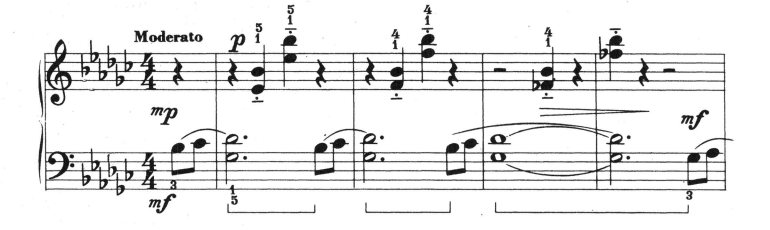

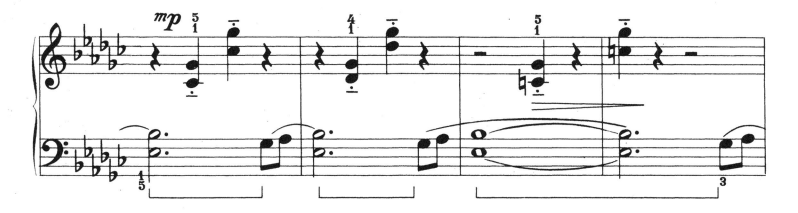

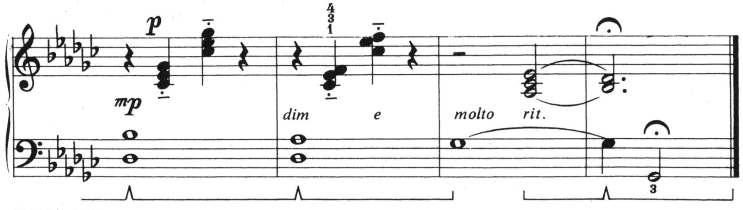

W. M. Co., 9586

FLUTE SONG AND DANCE

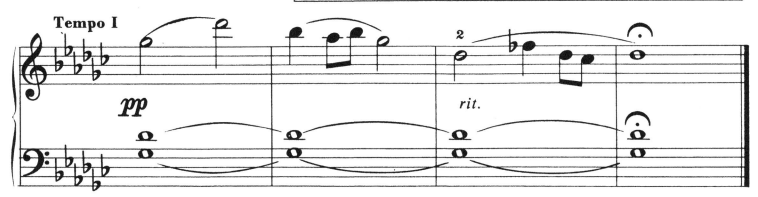

ON THE MISSISSIPPI

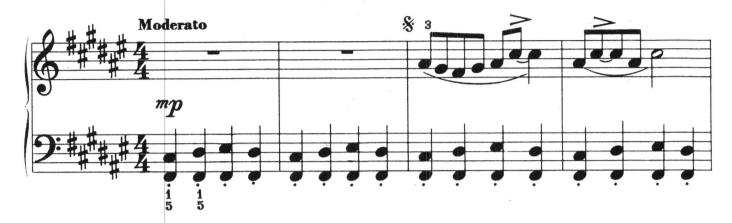

D.S. al fine

49

INSTRUCTIONS

1. Cut out the note cards.
2. Place each C on its corresponding piano key.
3. Place each G on its corresponding piano key.
4. Name a 2nd up and down from each C and G, and place the note cards on the corresponding piano keys.
5. Name the keys you have not covered. Place the remaining note cards on these keys.

DAILY PRACTICE SPEED TEST

Place all the note cards correctly in one minute.

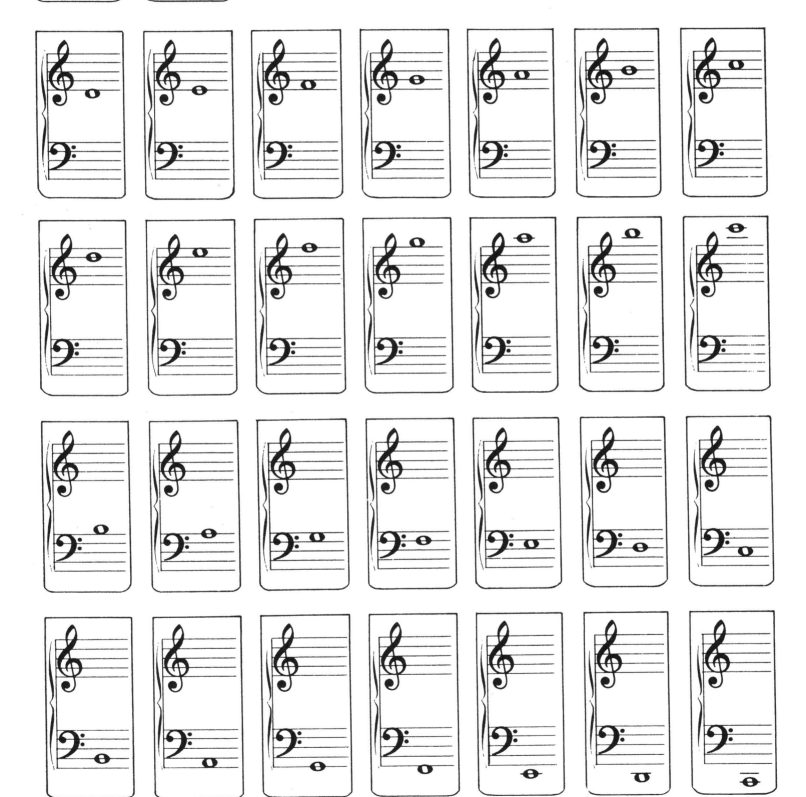

W. M. Co., 9586

MUSIC FROM
William Gillock

Available exclusively from

WILLIS MUSIC

"The Gillock name spells magic to teachers around the world..."
Lynn Freeman Olson, renowned piano pedagogue

NEW ORLEANS JAZZ STYLES
Gillock believed that every student's musical education should include experiences in a variety of popular stylings, including jazz, as a recurring phase of his or her studies. Students should also be encouraged to deviate from the written notes with their own improvisations if desired, for spontaneity is an essential ingredient of the jazz idiom.

Originals

NEW ORLEANS JAZZ STYLES
00415931 Book Only............................$5.99

MORE NEW ORLEANS JAZZ STYLES
00415946 Book Only............................$5.99

STILL MORE NEW ORLEANS JAZZ STYLES
00404401 Book Only............................$5.99

NEW ORLEANS JAZZ STYLES - COMPLETE
00416922 Book/Audio...........................$19.99

Duets *(arr. Glenda Austin)*

NEW ORLEANS JAZZ STYLES DUETS
00416805 Book/CD..............................$9.99

MORE NEW ORLEANS JAZZ STYLES DUETS
00416806 Book/CD..............................$9.99

STILL MORE NEW ORLEANS JAZZ STYLES DUETS
00416807 Book/CD..............................$9.99

Simplified *(arr. Glenda Austin)*

SIMPLIFIED NEW ORLEANS JAZZ STYLES
00406603 ....$5.99

MORE SIMPLIFIED NEW ORLEANS JAZZ STYLES
00406604 ....$5.99

STILL MORE SIMPLIFIED NEW ORLEANS JAZZ STYLES
00406605 ....$5.99

ACCENT ON GILLOCK SERIES
Excellent piano solos in all levels by Gillock. Great recital pieces!
00405993	Volume 1 Book	$5.99
00405994	Volume 2 Book	$5.99
00405995	Volume 3 Book	$5.99
00405996	Volume 4 Book	$5.99
00405997	Volume 5 Book	$5.99
00405999	Volume 6 Book	$5.99
00406000	Volume 7 Book	$5.99
00406001	Volume 8 Book	$5.99

ACCENT ON CLASSICAL
Early to Mid-Intermediate Level
Gillock transformed several classical favorites into accessible teaching pieces, including Beethoven's "Für Elise" and "German Dance" (Op.17/9). Other pieces in this timeless collection include: Capriccietto • Barcarolle • Piece in Classic Style • Sonatina in C.
00416932 ....$8.99

ACCENT ON DUETS
Mid to Later Intermediate Level
Eight fantastic Gillock duets in one book! Includes: Sidewalk Cafe • Liebesfreud (Kreisler) • Jazz Prelude • Dance of the Sugar Plum Fairy (Tchaikovsky) • Fiesta Mariachi. A must-have for every piano studio.
00416804 1 Piano/4 Hands......................$12.99

00415712	Accent on Analytical Sonatinas	EI	$5.99
00415797	Accent on Black Keys	MI	$5.99
00415748	Accent on Majors	LE	$5.99
00415569	Accent on Majors & Minors	EI	$5.99
00415165	Accent on Rhythm & Style	MI	$5.99

ACCENT ON SOLOS – COMPLETE
33 Pieces for the Advancing Young Pianist
A newly edited and engraved compilation of all 3 of Gillock's popular Accent on Solos books. These 33 short teaching pieces have been in print for over 50 years for a simple reason: the music continues to motivate piano students of every age!
00200896 Early to Later Elementary..............$12.99

ACCENT ON TWO PIANOS
Four Original Pieces for 2 Pianos, 4 Hands
Titles: Carnival in Rio • On a Paris Boulevard • Portrait of Paris • Viennese Rondo. Includes a duplicate score insert for the second piano.

00146176 Intermediate to Advanced $9.99

ALSO AVAILABLE

FOUNTAIN IN THE RAIN
A sophisticated Gillock classic! Composed in 1960, this piece is reminiscent of impressionism and continues to be on annual recital lists. Students particularly enjoy the changing harmonies and nailing the splashy cadenza in the middle!
00414908..$3.99
00114960 Duet, arr. Glenda Austin $3.99

PORTRAIT OF PARIS
This beautiful composition evokes the romance of long-ago Paris, its eighth notes building gracefully to an incredibly satisfying climax of cascading notes. Excellent for bringing out top-voicing. Gillock has also written a second piano part that results in a very effective piano duo arrangement.
00414627...$2.99

THREE JAZZ PRELUDES
These preludes may be played as a set or as individual pieces. These dazzling pieces are Gillock at his best.
00416100...$3.99

CLASSIC PIANO REPERTOIRE – WILLIAM GILLOCK
Newly engraved and edited!

00416912 Intermediate to Advanced $12.99
00416957 Elementary $8.99

WILLIAM GILLOCK RECITAL COLLECTION
Features an extensive compilation of over 50 of William Gillock's most popular and frequently performed recital pieces. Newly engraved and edited to celebrate Gillock's centennial year.

00201747 Intermediate to Advanced $19.99

WILLIS MUSIC

HAL•LEONARD®

Find us online at
www.willispianomusic.com